Fabulous Food

Sing Along — Tune: The Farmer in the Dell

Jo Cleland

Rourke Educational Media

rourkeeducationalmedia.com

Teacher Notes available at rem4teachers.com

© 2013 Rourke Educational Media

All rights reserved. No part of this book may be reproduced or utilized in any form or by any means, electronic or mechanical including photocopying, recording, or by any information storage and retrieval system without permission in writing from the publisher.

www.rourkeeducationalmedia.com

PHOTO CREDITS: Cover: , Title Page, 21: © Catherine Yeulet; Page 3: © Marilyn Nieves; Page 4: © Ina Peters; Page 5: © Carmen Martínez Banús; Page 6: © Jani Bryson; Page 7: © Troels Graugaard; Page 8: © Christopher Futcher; Page 9: © Marilyn Gould; Page 10: © Martinturzak; Page 11: © wael hamdan; Page 12: © PHALANO; Page 13: © Juriah Mosin; Page 14: © Annette Boettcher; Page 15: © Yuko Hirao; Page 16: © ALEAIMAGE; Page 17: © Mircea_dfa; Page 18: © Adauto Araujo; Page 19: © Sean Locke; Page 20: © Dejan Ristovski; Page 22

Editor: Precious McKenzie

Cover and Page design by Tara Raymo

Library of Congress PCN Data

Fabulous Food / Jo Cleland
(Sing and Read, Healthy Habits K-2)
ISBN 978-1-61810-084-9 (hard cover) (alk. paper)
ISBN 978-1-61810-217-1 (soft cover)
Library of Congress Control Number: 2011944394

Rourke Educational Media
Printed in the United States of America,
North Mankato, Minnesota

Rourke Educational Media

rourkeeducationalmedia.com
customerservice@rourkeeducationalmedia.com • PO Box 643328 Vero Beach, Florida 32964

Start song
The Farmer in the Dell

What makes bones grow?
What makes teeth grow?

Milk and **yogurt**, cream and cheese.

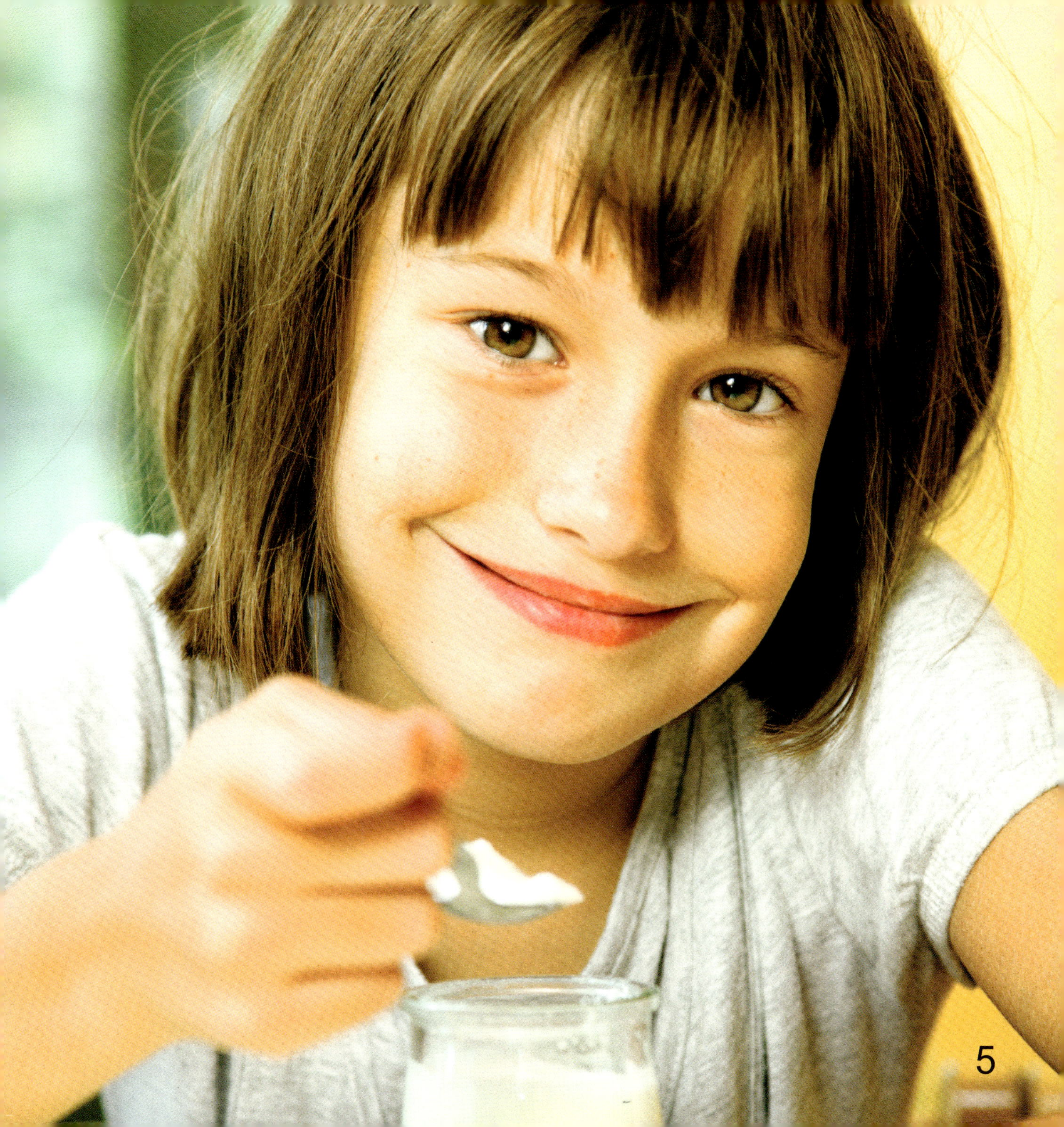

Calcium makes them grow.

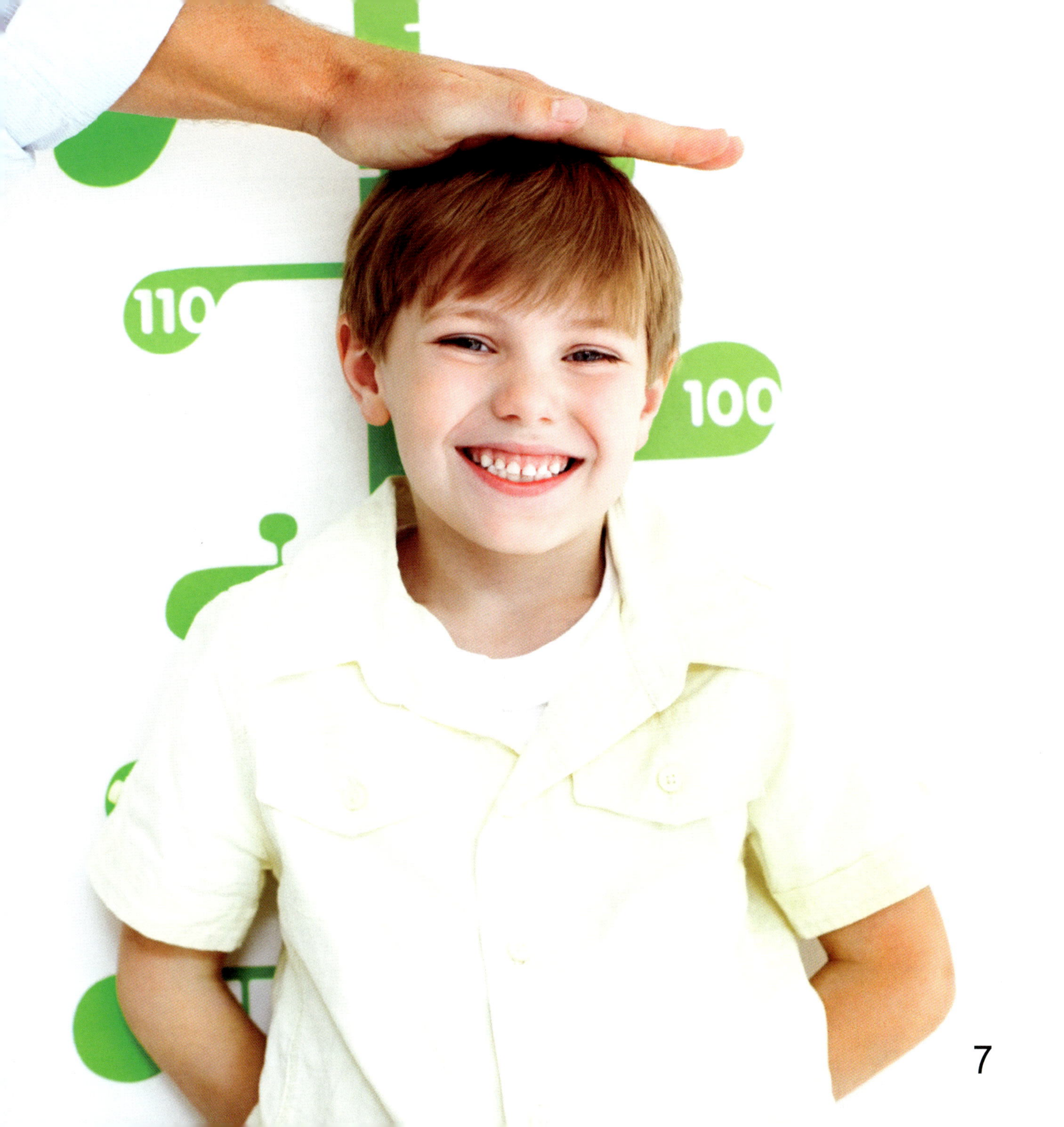
110
100

What makes blood strong?

What makes **muscles** strong?

Fish and spinach, nuts and eggs.

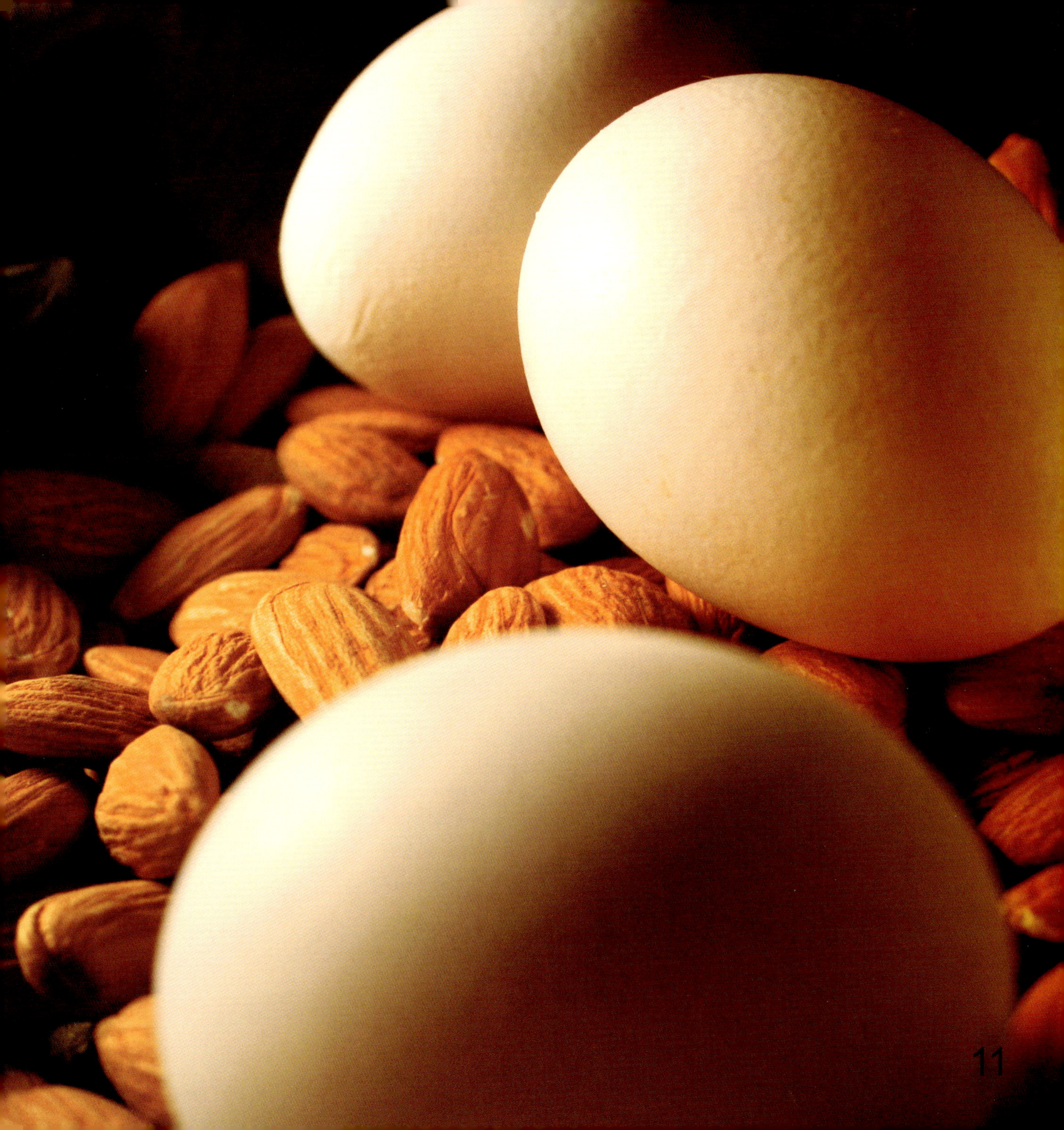

Protein makes them strong.

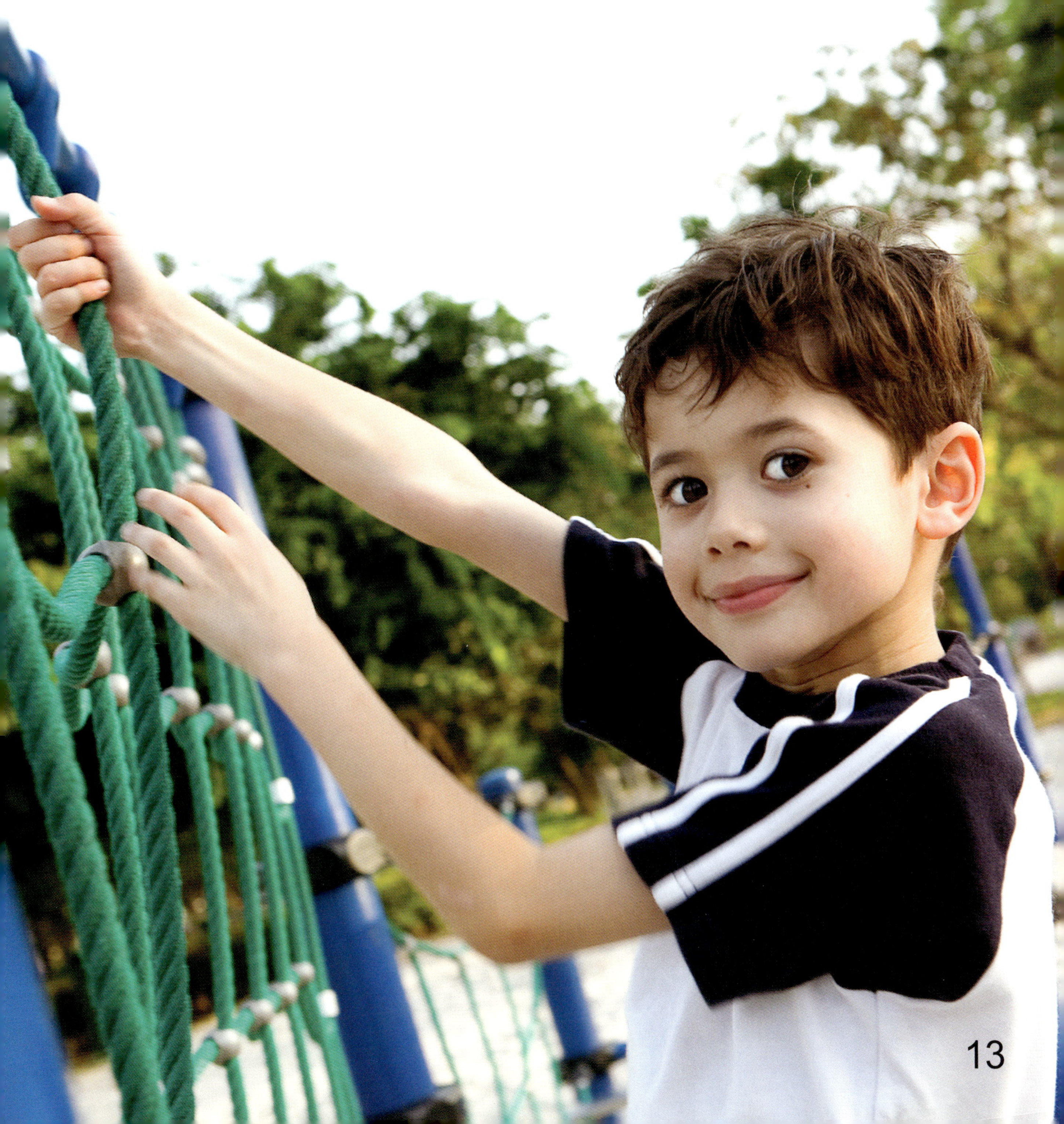

Why can we move well?

Why can we breathe well?

Wheat and rice, oats and corn.

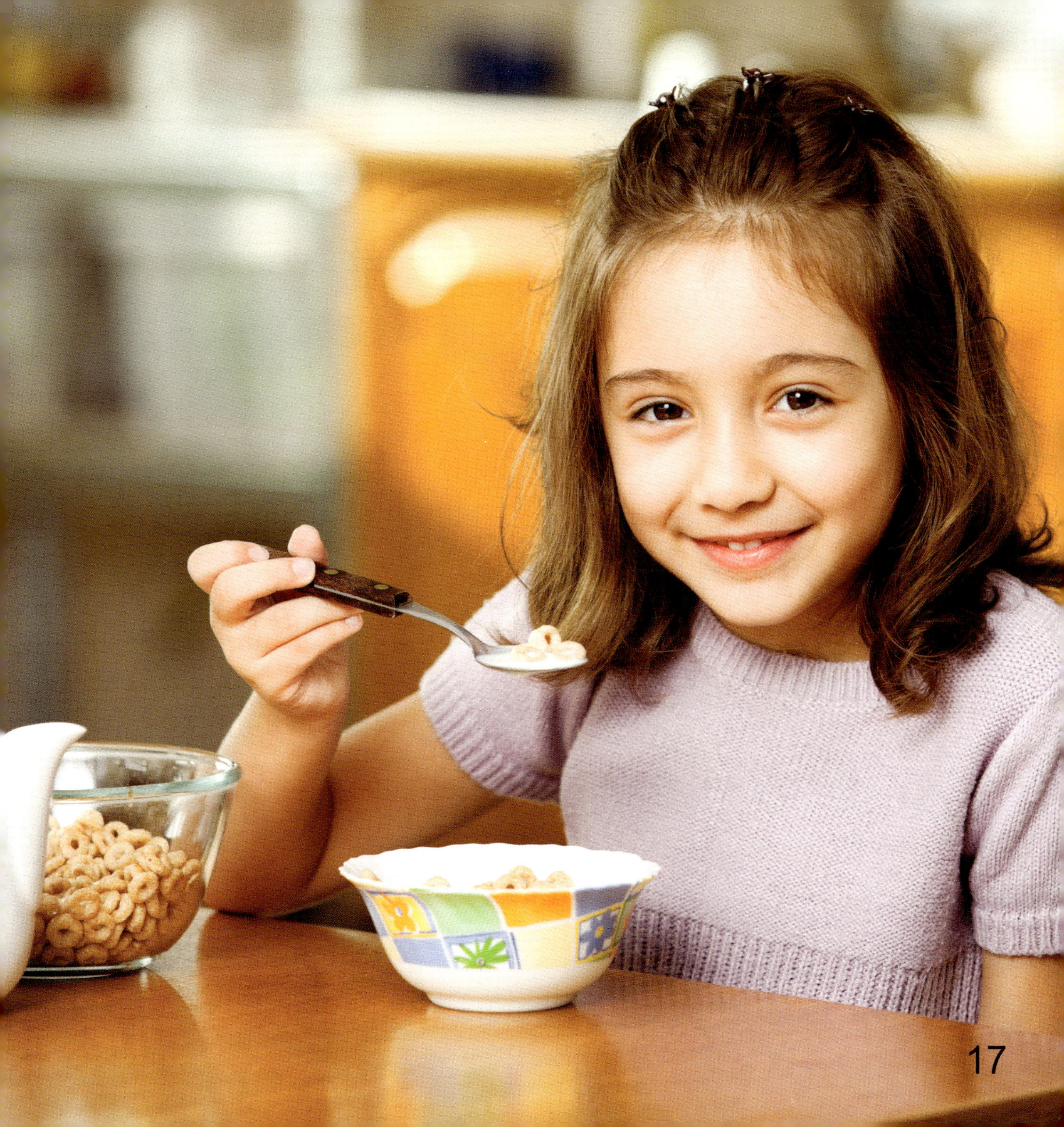

Carbohydrates keep us well.

19

We know what to eat, fruits, veggies, bread, and meat.

Fab, fab, fabulous food.
Now let's all go and eat!

Glossary

calcium (KAL-see-uhm): a soft, white metal

carbohydrates (kar-boh-HYE-drates): energy food

muscles (MUHSS-uhlz): rope-like parts on the inside of your body that make your body move

protein (PROH-teen): strength food

yogurt (YOH-gurt): a creamy food made from milk

Song Lyrics

Fabulous Food
Tune: The Farmer in the Dell

What makes bones grow?
What makes teeth grow?
Milk and yogurt, cream
 and cheese.
Calcium makes them grow.

What makes blood strong?
What makes muscles strong?
Fish and spinach, nuts and eggs.
Protein makes them strong.

Why can we move well?
Why can we breathe well?
Wheat and rice, oats and corn.
Carbohydrates keep us well.

We know what to eat,
fruits, veggies, bread, and meat.
Fab, fab, fabulous food.
Now let's all go and eat!

Index

bones   3

calcium   6

carbohydrates   18

muscles   9

protein   12

teeth   3

Websites

familyfun.go.com/recipes/cooking-with-kids/

www.nutritionexplorations.org/kids.php

www.choosemyplate.gov/kids/

About the Author

Jo Cleland enjoys writing books, composing songs, and making games. She loves to read, sing, and play games with children.

Ask The Author!
www.rem4students.com